A FATHER'S GUIDE TO EMBRACING AND ENJOYING

THEIR SPECIAL NEEDS CHILD!

By Daniel Randall Jr.

Copyright

Quantity Sales. Special discounts are available in quantity purchases by corporations, associations, networking groups. For details contact www.SelfPublishedAuthorsNetwork the address above

Individual Sales-

Want to know more about what I do. Contact me @

drandallcc12hbu@sbcglobal.com

Includes biographical references and index

Contents

DEDICATION

Thoroughly Immersed: A father's guide to enjoying and enriching the life of a special needs child. This is *"My side of the story"* of how a man copes with having a special needs child. Why am I writing this book? It's because I want the same people in my situation to be encouraged. One dad told me, the parents need to know what to do. You can take this pain and turn it into power; A powerful testimony.

This book is being written for the parents of special needs children. The ones who feel the pain that comes after that first diagnosis. The ones who feel that pain and wonder, "What now?" There is a pain that paralyzes your soul. One wonderful mother describes it as "a pain so great it is as if someone strikes you in the heart with a baseball bat!" This is the story of my pain which is a constant challenge. I was one of the people asking *"How this could happen to me?"*

I have found out there is a strength we find from our pain. In this experience comes humility like no other, found through prayer and focus. This is my story of overcoming having a son diagnosed with Autism. The Bible says *"When a man is converted, then he is to strengthen his brothers"* (Luke 22:32). Having my special needs son changed me, convicted me for my "Alpha Male" way of thinking and converted me.

This experience has humbled me and that is why I am so passionate to share my experiences and my advice on raising a special needs child. I'm excited to share with you how you can enjoy and be enriched by raising your special needs child. I want to encourage others in my situation. GOD knew who he was giving these children to. You can turn the pain of Autism into a Powerful testimony. My Purpose, my assignment is to show you how.

"Glory to God in the Highest and Peace to his People on Earth!" This book is dedicated to my wife Beryl, My Daughter Danielle and My Son Daniel. It is also dedicated to Daniel's caregiver, Wilynthia Moore. The love you have for Daniel is heaven sent. You mean the world to us.

Special thanks to David "Big Dave" Haynes who is Daniel's godfather and lifelong barber. I will always cherish the patience and love you have for my son.

Thanks to the late Bishop Arthur Brazier, pastor emeritus of Apostolic Church of God. I was never a member of your church, but your words of wisdom during our counseling session began my conviction. Thanks to mom, Clara Randall, aka Nana. Your presence has made a lifetime of a difference.

Finally, thanks to the Men of Omega Psi Phi (Roo to the Bruhs!) and all the teachers, coaches, and village keepers who have helped me and my family raise our special needs child in a loving, nurturing environment.

FOREWORD

I have had the honor of knowing Daniel Randall II, aka "Danny" since our high school days. He has always been a leader, whether on the football field for the "Mighty Mendel Monarchs" in high school, on the mean streets of Chicago as a police officer creating a different impression contrary to what we see on the news, or as the "servant leader" in his home showing that a black man can be committed to his marriage and the rearing of his children.

I have a special sense of gratitude for Danny for allowing me to help "Tell His Story" of coming to grips with embracing and enjoying raising a child with special needs like his son, Daniel. It is a story that not only needed, but necessary. Every man, whether young or old, married or single, with children or about consider having them needs to hear.

Danny speaks from the heart on his experience in being a father dealing with raising a child with autism. He shares the trials and triumphs. He shares the setbacks as well as the successes from a "man's point of view" speaking directly to men and the women who love them.

Raising any child comes with its own set of challenges and discovery, but those challenges are exponentially heightened when you add in mental and physical disabilities.

Danny provides thoughtful and insightful steps in this book to help fathers cope with the challenges, overcome the obstacles and discover the 'hidden treasures" inside of children like Danny that can't be seen on the surface.

He provides tools and strategies that anyone can implement right away to start seeing positive changes in the way you can relate to your child, encourage your child and advocate within the community for better understanding and support of your special needs child.

If you've been struggling as a father in dealing with your special needs child, Danny has supplied the answers just for you! Get ready for a new journey towards Embracing and Enjoying raising your child. It's going to be an UNSTOPPABLE ride!

Terrance "The Unstoppable Coach" Leftridge
Amazon Best Selling Author of the book "You Are Unstoppable"
Accountability Coach and Transformational Speaker
Unstoppable Coaching Services

INTRODUCTION

My name is Danny Randall Jr. In the fall of 2002, I could not be more in love with life because I worked in two fields that I had a great passion for. By day, I was a football coach at LindblomHigh School in the West Englewood neighborhood on the south side of Chicago. At night, I was a Chicago Police Officer patrolling the city.

I was exactly what you wanted in a coach. I was demanding, competitive, driven and quite effective. The high school was happy to have me because Lindblom did not win one game the season before I arrived! When I arrived in 2002, went undefeated that season until losing to John Hope High School in the Intra City Championship 6-0. I was also an effective, productive police officer who loved his job

These two professions suited my aggressive, decisive and "willing to take charge" personality. I was the typical "ALPHA MALE" and I loved who I was (*Maybe a little too much*)! I would often blast out loud from my CD player a song by R. Kelly and JAY-Z called "The Best of Both Worlds".

At the same time, I had a loving wife and 2 healthy, strong and wonderful kids in Danielle and Daniel. Yes life couldn't get much better! I was on "top of the world" and I had no idea what was coming next. You see, GOD sent something my way that humbled me and brought this "ALPHA MALE" down to his knees. In the fall of 2002, **my son was diagnosed with Autism.** My world was rocked and never would be the same again.

The Back Story:

My son's name is Daniel Vernon Randall III. I am a Daniel Vernon Randall Jr. They call me Danny, my son Daniel. My wife Beryl calls him Dan. His sister calls him "Big Boy". Daniel is more of an affirmative name. Danny is an abbreviation. When you have a special needs son, there is a need to maintain that authority and affirmative designation. You are constantly teaching, constantly redirecting and constantly learning. I think I call him Daniel because that is more formal.

He was born November 11, 2000. That day for me was UNREAL! It was amazing! I didn't know at that time he was a special needs child and we didn't know we would have a son before this day. It was numbing. It was such a shock that I just dropped to my knees.

It was an indescribable feeling. I hoped growing up that I would have kids. I hoped to find the right person, get married and have a healthy child. I already had a daughter at this time by the name of Danielle (currently

17yrs old), but to now have a son, and a big boy at that, was mind boggling.

It was about 2 yrs after his birth that Daniel was diagnosed with Autism. At first, there was no indication. Daniel was a healthy, handsome boy and I was on "cloud nine". But as he grew, Beryl (who is a nurse) and I noticed he was slow to speak. We had him tested and one of the doctors told us he had Autism.

What is Autism?

According to the Centers for Disease Control and Prevention (CDC), Autism spectrum disorder (ASD) is a group of developmental disabilities that can cause significant social, communication and behavioral challenges.

Dr. Amanda Carter, contributing clinical consultant and CEO /Founder of Care and Recreational Activities For Autistic People (CARAFAP) defines Autism as a complex developmental disability that impacts and impairs one's reciprocal social interaction, verbal and nonverbal communication skills, executive functioning, imaginative skills, activities and interest, fine motor skills, adaptive living, and independence.

Autism is a speech and communicative delay with serious with serious behaviors and sensory issues. The child has social and communication delays.   This condition affects a growing number of young boys more so than girls.

Dr. Carter reports that one in every 68 children is diagnosed with autism, and it is said that more than 3.5 million Americans live with an Autism Spectrum Diagnosis. Boys are four times more likely than girls to develop autism, and the causes of this disparity are unknown. According to CDC, 1 in 42 boys carry a diagnosis of autism, 4.5 times as many as girls.

I remember saying to the doctor, "Fix It"! Yeah I said that and the doctor said back to me that you just can't "FIX" autism.   I didn't have a clue what autism was at that time. It was like someone speaking a foreign language to me.   It was mind boggling.   See, I'm a police officer and in my mind, if there is a problem you fix it. Maybe that's my "Alpha Male "way of thinking. When the doctor said you just can't fix it, I felt a powerful pain take over me. One parent described it as if "someone took a baseball bat and hit you in the back!"

At the present time there is no cure, which makes this condition quite mysterious. Many causes of autism proposed include genetics, immunizations, environmental influences, nutrition, prenatal and postnatal environments, autoimmune disease, amygdala neurons, lead, mercury, viral infections, Vitamin D deficiency, and being born to geriatric parents.

The learning, thinking, and problem-solving abilities of people with ASD can range from gifted to severely challenged. Some people with ASD need a lot of help in their daily lives; others need less.

A diagnosis of ASD now includes several conditions that used to be diagnosed separately: autistic disorder, pervasive developmental disorder not otherwise specified (PDD-NOS), and Asperger syndrome. These conditions are now all called autism spectrum disorder.

People with ASD often have problems with social, emotional, and communication skills.

They might repeat certain behaviors and might not want change in their daily activities. Many people with ASD also have different ways of learning, paying attention, or reacting to things. Signs of ASD begin during early childhood and typically last throughout a person's life. We do know early intervention is the key. I know in time new research will come and more breakthroughs are coming.

Having a child like Daniel is like having a HUGE treasure chest with a padlock on it. Do you focus on the lock or on the treasure that lies inside? It's like cracking a safe. You got to constantly stay at it and overcome it. There is an Extraordinary Gift inside of your child, but it's up to the parent to find it and pull it out. Any child is a "gift from GOD" whether they are A-typical or not. It's important to enjoy them, enrich them and encourage them as much as you can.

But before we go more into the parenting aspect, let me tell you about my childhood. It forms a basis for *HOW and WHY* I raise Daniel the way I do.

16

THE BEGINNING: MY CHILDHOOD

My childhood could only be described as "The Childhood from Heaven!" My parents, Daniel Randall Sr. and Clara Randall, made it crystal clear that my siblings and I were loved. We were loved fiercely and disciplined fiercely. Both of them were quite progressive. My father was a mechanic for the CTA and my mom was a postal manager.

The earliest memories of my childhood begin with my father carrying over his shoulder while taking me to work with him. We lived on 79th street & Union on the south side of Chicago and we would walk down to the Chicago Transit Authority (CTA) bus garage where he worked as a mechanic. We traveled this route every day, but one day during our daily walk, I remember him taking me into the currency exchange on 79th and Vincennes. He placed me on the counter and called some men over telling them, "Look at my son! He is going to be someone out here!"

I don't know if he knew them or not, but the men gathered around me and smiled. This was during a time when black men, although they did not know each other, they acknowledged each other. Moments like this made me feel special and loved. I realized at that time that I was his pride and joy, his own trophy per se.

The men gathered around, smiled and nodded their heads in approval. On this day, one gentleman in particular with an unforgettable twinkle in his eyes stated, "That little guy is built like Jim Brown!" When my father first placed me on that counter and gathered the men around, I felt afraid but after that comment I could not feel more safe and secure.

As a child, I truly felt loved. I was blessed with encouraging parents; sometimes a little too much. They had a way of making any small task that we completed seem as though it was the greatest event they had ever seen! The period that I grew up in was without a doubt the greatest time to be a black child. I had the "childhood from heaven".

We were able to play an assortment of sports and childhood games. We were what you would call "upper middle class" (at least that's what they told me). My parents were only in their 20's and owned a two flat building on the 7600 block of south Loomis. This was the early 70s which was very good for that period in time and even today.

I remember in the summer of 1976, my father had this ritual. He would pull out both of the Cadillac's (one tan, the other blue) out of the garage into the alley. Once enough neighbors would come down, he would start to wash both of them. My father was a tall, boisterous man who loved to show off. We took pride in living like "The Joneses".

I also mentioned that my parents disciplined me fiercely. They believed in discipline (whooping, spankings) as a way to rear me properly. That is something in my opinion that is lacking in families today. Because they both disciplined me, there are things I never did again. I never knew if the punishment would come from my mom, my dad or both of them. But to this day, I remember and respect the discipline I received from my parents because it showed me I was loved.

I grew up healthy and had no concept of anything such as *Autism*. I was my parent's trophy, healthy and happy. That is the relationship that I have created with my son Daniel.

MY EDUCATION: THE MOLD FOR MY ASSSIGNMENT—

S t. Sabina Grade School, MENDEL Catholic HS, & LINCOLN University.

St. Sabina was a school that simply instilled discipline in me which in turn would bring about confidence. The discipline was first instilled by the nuns there and my God they did not spare the rod! Neither did the Gym teachers. They had the "**Green Light to *spank* you**" if you got out of line which instilled fear in me.

In those days, there were consequences for your actions and you accountable, unlike today. We didn't live in a "Litigious Society" where a growing number of people do not want to be accountable for their own actions and they want someone else to foot the bill or pay for the mistakes. Our society back in the day produced" a better kind of people".

I have an obsession with the way I was raised and disciplined at home and school. I was blessed to be able to participate in football during my 7th and 8th grade years. These years would instill a great deal of confidence inside of me. Under Mr. Thornton, our Head Coach in 7th grade and Hank Mosley, a former Chicago Bears player, we overwhelmed our opponents. During the football season of 1977, I was blessed to be part of a winning team that put up ridiculous numbers. Our record during the regular season was 10-1.

That one loss I would not experience because I missed the first two games due to pneumonia. We registered 6 shut outs and the kids we played simply could not score on us! We had one running back named Vashon Morgan who had 40 plus touchdowns that year and another back named Bruce Abrons had 20 plus touchdowns.

We were so overwhelming because of the discipline structure we had and that success made me confident. Vashon also is the dad of a special needs child and a great one I can add. We both feel the discipline structure and instilling confidence is important in raising our children.

To this day Vashon and I are still close; even more so because of our beautiful special needs sons. Vashon was the star running back and I took pride in being his blocker or enforcer. It gave me a sense of identity that I have to this day; a protective nature that I feel in my heart.

My involvement in the game of football during my grade school years helped mold my character. I played the position of offensive guard and my job was to protect and sacrifice myself for my smaller quarterback and running back teammates.

They would be the ones gaining more attention for scoring or running or throwing the football. St. Sabina developed my confidence and character and those skills are with me to this day.

Because of our success, we were recruited by the nationally acclaimed sports conference, The Chicago Catholic League for their programs. Vashon would accept an offer from Mount Carmel High School while I went to Mendel College Preparatory High School. That would make us rivals all through high school.

The times I had in high school were so amazing I decided to keep a diary because at times I was not sure the fun I had was actually happening to me. Playing football at Mendel instilled leadership in me that would mold me to being the advocator I needed to be for my son. My coach, Pete Thanos, and the staff created an environment that developed my traits. *A leader is one who sets direction and help themselves and others do what is needed to move forward,* but it begins with a person who is willing to take the initiative to help their child strive in this world as best as they can.

I graduated from Mendel in 1982. I would attend Mount Scenario in Ladysmith where I would play football my freshman year but left after a year because, although the team would win the conference, I craved to play at a higher level of college play. I did not get the guidance necessary coming out of high school.

I was not highly recruited but still had a desire to play. I attended Olive Harvey Community College the fall of 1983 because I had not chosen a college to continue playing football. I spent hours in the weight room at Olive Harvey and it was there where a "chance meeting" occurred that would change my life.

A couple of days before Thanksgiving in 1983, I would walk in the weight room to begin my workout. Three young men noticed me working out alone and they seemed somewhat impressed. One of these young men asked me where I played college football because they thought I Looked the part.

My words to them were "I am looking for a school to play now!" That's when they told me they attended Lincoln University in Jefferson Missouri. After a short conversation, I struck up a fast friendship with these three young men that like most of my chance encounters continue to this very day.

Lincoln U would instill in me the necessities to ready me for my assigned task. I would acquire the traits of Manhood and Scholarship. On 12/6/86, I would pledge "Omega Psi Phi Fraternity" where "Perseverance and Uplift" were the cardinal principles. Lincoln U would also be instrumental in meeting another young man whose name is Marcellus McFadden.

You see, Mark is very important to me because he pledged" Omega" with me and now he also is the father of a special needs son. It's amazing how God placed these young men in my life as friends and our assignments in the rearing of our sons unifies us even more. The friendships I developed at Lincoln where fast and enduring as well.

So how did the things I learned and received during my childhood help me now on this journey to embracing and enjoying caring for my special needs child? Well as I share 8 tips with you later in this book, you will see how having incredible parents who had their own flaws allowed me to become the father I am today. You will see how discipline and structure have become necessary in my own life as well as a critical tool in raising a special needs child.

My childhood taught me the true value of Manhood, Scholarship, Perseverance and Patience. These are skills I use daily in helping Daniel become a better young man despite some of his limitations. The way I say "I love You Daniel" every day comes from that love I received during my childhood.

I am dedicated to my all of my children, not just Daniel who is the subject of this book. That was the hardest skill to obtain however, because as I grew older, I lost the model in my life that was supposed to teach me dedication. You see, the one man who cherished me as a trophy growing up became the very man I despised as a young man.

Thoroughly Immersed

MY RELATIONSHIP WITH MY FATHER (THE CONFLICT)

Danny Randall Sr. was a "Real man"! He was an "ALPHA Male"! He was a man of constant praise. He was fun loving, affectionate and never cowered. I got my "Alpha Male" personality from my father. My father didn't have a "book" to raise me, but he knew what he was doing in raising me. I was rambunctious and needed a little more attention than my siblings. That's why I stayed in catholic school so long.

He was awesome up to the age of 12 yrs. old, and then the conflict started. My father became involved with another woman who used him. She had a history of being a "Black Widow" and my father became smitten with her. He moved in with the woman who eventually got him to quit his job and then she kicked him out. My father tried to come back home, but my mother wasn't having it! It came to the point one day that my father set the back porch on fire in an attempt to get my mother to open the door.

This was a turning point in my life. I was so mad at my father that I ran out the door and charged him wrestling him to the ground. I remember the fire fighters pulling me off of him. This incident changed me because I had to RISE UP against this man that I once adored.

There was a time I praised this man and enjoyed playing ball with this man, but now I despised him. From the age of 12 until 14, my opinion of him slowly and painfully changed. He was once revered like a "god" by me and this period of time devastated me. I had little contact with him since then and had no remorse when he passed away.

Seeing what happened to my father makes me fiercer in my actions towards my children. I saw what happened to a man who abandoned his responsibility and I didn't want that to happen to me. I'm driven by the FEAR of what might happen if I shrink from my responsibilities. I remember a time when my daughter reminded me that I forgot to bring her lunch to school. She said, "Daddy, you forgot to bring me my lunch!" Oh that rocked me to my core! She has never gone hungry a day in her life, but still the thought of not taking care of my children was numbing.

This was a fundamental shift in the way this "ALPHA Male" thought about life and it is part of the reason I wrote this book. Having a "special needs child" made me change the way I thought. Most men want a son that is in "his image". When that didn't happen, I had to evolve and humble myself so that I could be able to care for my child.

I had to be responsible. I had to be there for him. I had to make sure the bills for treatment were paid, so I worked 3 jobs at one point.

I reflected on my dad when Daniel was born November 11, 2000. A calming joy came over me because now I had a son that I knew I would never abandon. I knew what not to do in raising my son and daughter. I was made a better father thru the conflict I went thru with my father. It engrained in me what happens when a man shrinks from his responsibilities. However, my convictions would be tested once Daniel turned 2 yrs. old.

THE DIAGNOSIS

When we got the diagnosis of autism, I was devastated. The calming joy had turned into anger. "Why did this happen to me?" I thought I had the "perfect family" with a wife, a daughter and now a son! "I'm an ALPHA male! "How could I possibly have a son like this?" I blamed my wife telling her this had to come from her side of the family!

I was in an "avoidance and denial" stage when I first learned of Daniel's diagnosis. I avoided dealing with his situation by hanging out at night and staying away from the family. I denied the situation existed because I didn't want to deal with my failed expectations for my son.

I felt trapped! I knew I couldn't leave, but I had no idea how to deal with this. How would the other "ALPHA Male" friends I hung out with view my "special needs son"? I didn't really talk about it to my friends. There was a denial.

I began coaching football at the time, partying all the time and avoiding the situation. I remember my wife telling me "You're leaving us after your son is slipping into another world!" I had a myriad of emotions and nobody knew what I was going thru. I felt like I couldn't talk to anyone.

This diagnosis of Autism was now ripping my "perfect family" apart. Danielle bore the brunt of my anger. I would say random things to her and my wife that were nasty. No child should have been subjected to that, but I was embarrassed. My Alpha male, football coach persona couldn't handle it. I wanted my boy to "Fit in" just like my girl did. Every father wants that for their son.

Per Dr. Carter of CARAFAP, stress in parents has become a subject of research, as parents play a major role in managing treatment of children with autism, and as a result these stressors may impair one's ability to conduct optimal oversight over children and adolescents. It's important for men to know that there is someone to talk to.

There is need for this book and I wish I had this book when I first went thru this journey. Men need to lean on others and GOD to immerse themselves in the need of their "special needs children". Men have to learn to let things out and share their feelings about being a father of a "special needs child".

I would like to share with you "8 Tips" I have learned over the course of raising my son. These tips range from advocating for the rights of special needs children, enjoying the journey as well as self care for you as a father.

The 8 Tips!

Tip #1:   Form a Relationship with GOD

The only way you can make it through this thing is by prayer and forming a relationship with GOD. For me, I had to go to "My CHAMBER". That's where I go to pray. It's a dark, peaceful place where I can go and block out all the problems in the world. It's a virtual place wrapped in spiritual relevance. There was a time I went to the "chamber" in order to deal with my son's behavior. Daniel was around 7 or 8 years old and he just couldn't sit still in class. It got so bad that the teachers would physically barricade him in a section of the classroom. I was at my wits end!

One day I just decided to go into Daniel's room with him. I turned off all the lights so it would be dark in there. I wanted it to be just me, Daniel and GOD! I got down on my hands and knees and started praying! All of the sudden, a peace I can't explain came over me and the room. Another time, I sat in the car in the garage with Daniel and we listened to the song "Take Me to the King" by Tamela Mann.

The peace we felt at that moment caused me to break down in tears and made me realize this one thing. For every earthly problem there has got to be an earthly solution. You just got to take it to a higher power and allow Him to help you figure it out. But first you have to get quiet, listen to that "inner voice" and that's where you'll find the answers to dealing with your special needs child.

After I spend time with GOD, I get a sense of peace and humility. Forming a relationship with GOD is like having a "manufacturer's warranty". If anything goes wrong with an item, you can always call the manufacturer for assistance. The same is true for Father's dealing with raising their special needs children. You need to go back to the manufacturer, i.e. GOD to find the solutions. When I talk to the manufacturer OF Daniel ABOUT Daniel, I always come back with a solution as well as a "peace of mind" necessary to continue this journey with him.

I look at other parents of special needs children that have mastered this tip. They have an "aura of serenity". They have a sense of clarity that is unbelievable. It's spiritual! After coming out of "My Chamber", I have been able to set aside my anger and love Daniel more. I've been able to see Daniel for Daniel; not this child with special needs. I recognized that Daniel was *"an assignment from GOD!"* Fathers, recognize you were "Built for this!"

Everything I went through growing up and dealing with the issues with my father prepared for this moment. The pain, the uncertainty, the multitude of puzzle pieces that didn't seem to fit now makes sense. Fathers are looking at the "pieces of their unfinished puzzle" and wondering what to do next. Seek out GOD and form a relationship. Start with the ministers in your community.

I live in Chicago and it is mostly known for being the "Windy City" and the town of gangsters. However, Chicago also has some powerful ministers! Names like Rev. Jesse Jackson Sr., Father Michael Phleger, the late Bishop Arthur Brazier and Rev John Hannah. I remember hearing John Hannah say, "Anything you are going thru at the moment, you were anointed for that task." Fathers, you were chosen for this task with your child. You cannot run from it! So let GOD help you complete it.

The late Bishop Brazier was also instrumental in helping me as a father deal with my anger. I was angry. I was angry about my situation, I was angry with MY CHILD! How many fathers have felt that way in their lives? My Wife reached out to Bishop Brazier, who was the pastor of Apostolic Church of God in Christ where the membership at one time was over 20,000 people.

We weren't members and I lashed out at my wife for calling him. I told her, "He wasn't going to call us back! He doesn't even know us!" A few days later, he called! He called us into his office and when he met us, he asked us a lot of questions.

But one question stood out and caught us off guard! Bishop Brazier asked us, "When was the last time you two were intimate?" Here we are sitting in this palatial office with this "bigger than life preacher" and he asks us what?

What he was doing was asking us about intimacy. He knew we needed that. I was angry and my wife was confused as to why. Bishop Brazier essentially helped us in a profound way to forgive each other, lose the anger and realize intimacy is important. The anger I carried began to fall off and I was able to move forward.

The point here is that I couldn't have gotten that advice just from my friends or my "homies!" A man of GOD who has a relationship with GOD is the only one that can help fathers tap into the spiritual side and learn to deal with his special needs child in a different way. There are ministers all over the world willing to help you form a relationship with GOD so that you can have a better relationship with their special needs child.

$$\Omega$$

Use this section to reflect on what you have read thus far and how you can relate it to your own journey you're your own special needs children.

_____

_____

_____

_____

_____

Thoroughly Immersed

Thoroughly Immersed

TIP #2:   Treat Your Child Like a "Child"; Not a Special Needs Child!

On a father's journey to fully embracing and enjoying their "special needs child", it's important to remember that they still are children. Therefore, we should treat them like children. These children have the same need for new adventures. These children have the same sense of exploration. These children want to swing from the monkey bars, climb trees, go fishing, and play with toys just like other typical children.

Parents with special needs children don't fret over some of the things that parents with "typical or normal" children struggle with. Parents with special needs children need to develop more patience, strength and resolve.

Dr. Amanda Carter: "Although, parenting a child with special needs may feel like a marathon and an ongoing challenge; however, it is imperative to treat your children fairly, with integrity, dignity, and everlasting love. Although, children with autism may have higher challenges than neurotypical individuals they can sense nepotism and/or favoritism. Too often when this occurs, children will retaliate, act out with aggression and/or emotional dysregulation."

There is a devotion to your child that needs to be developed. In my opinion, parents of special needs children have more patience and strength than most other parents. When I became a parent of a child with special needs, there was humility and a strength that also came with being appointed with this task.

Get your children out in public. Get them around other "typical "children. Don't keep them closed in. Getting your children out into the world establishes a sense of belonging for your child. It also stimulates brain activity which is good for any child including special needs children. Find physical activities that your children enjoy. We take Daniel to swim classes, to the movies, out to dinner and even on simple walks in the parks. Daniel has a drum class during the week. The key is to get them engaged in some type of activity.

It was hard for me to try this at first. Daniel was about 9 years ago when we really started implementing this strategy. Because he has sensory issues, all the noises of certain and activities and some environments where there is close contact with other people could ultimately lead to "meltdowns" in children with this certain type of autism (Autism Spectrum Disorder).

Between the ages of 2 and 9 years old, we didn't actively pursue this ideal because we quite honestly weren't getting good advice. We had counselors, therapists and advisors that were telling us it was going to be tough dealing with Daniel's delays. The information they shared with us was unnerving and disappointing. These cognitive delays and sensory issues were going to be challenging.

But we had to recognize that "a Delay is NOT a Denial!" We could learn to accept the diagnosis WITHOUT surrendering to it. I refused to drop to my knees and let Autism enslave Daniel, me or the rest of the family! We decided as a family to accept Daniel's situation and deal with it. Just because Daniel had this disorder, it didn't mean he could not enjoy some of the same things that other typical children enjoy every day. The family just has to "stay in the fight!"

Special needs parents shouldn't feel like they have to tell people about their child's condition because it's none of their business! But now we know that people are willing to assist us when they know what the situation is. When we go to church, people assist us. When Daniel goes swimming, people assist us.

There was one time when one dad approached me and politely asked me about his condition. He said something to effect of getting Daniel socialized with other kids. After I pulled him to the side and explained his situation, my relationship with this man became stronger and he initially inspired me to write this book.

Physically, Daniel has never been sick a day in his life. He does have a speech pathologist (Dr. Brady) that works with him with his words and cognitive issues. The activities he is involved continues to improve his development. We are slowly integrating him into physical sports like wrestling and football and we are moving him out of the "therapeutic school environments". For some children, being in a therapeutic environment can be isolating. It's too inclusive in my opinion. It is helpful for a period of time, but if our special needs children are going to grow, they need to be in mainstream society.

Dr. Carter: Therapeutic schools for children with autism opposed to public education schools are situational and contingent upon an individual's need. However, students who tend to be lower functioning have a greater benefit of attending schools that offer intensive wrap around services which can ultimately improve their functional skills, personal development and enhancement. However, an individual who is higher functioning may have an opportunity to thrive and become successful in the real world if inclusive services are rendered. Inclusion in a classroom setting ensures opportunities for students with disabilities to learn alongside with non-disabled peers in general education classrooms. Although, they are included in the class additional accommodations and modifications are made.

While Daniel was in therapeutic school, we began to notice a regression in him. But once we decided to take the challenge and incorporating Daniel into mainstream activities, he began to flourish. I also found that inner city neighborhoods were best equipped to deal with special needs issues like autism. This is because there are many stressors going on at the same time in the inner city. People who see "special needs children" are not shocked by the behaviors because they see far worse in their communities on a daily basis.

I remember one time when I took Daniel to a mainstream swim pool in the Englewood community of Chicago. Daniel began to have a meltdown and everybody looked at me like I was the only one freaking out at this scene! The one little boy came up to me and said, "Mister, you want me to go and get him?"

The boy went over and talked to Daniel and everything turned out fine. I don't know what the boy said to Daniel, but he was able to handle it. This child was able to relate to him in a way some adults can't.

For the father reading this book, do regular father/child things with your children. Go for walks; play catch; run around with them; Go to the movies. Every child has a special talent, but you have to spend time with them to find it out. We found out that Daniel had an uncanny ability to swim under water for long periods of time without taking a breath. His swim coach (Rudolph Henry) is amazed at Daniel's ability to literally breathe through his nose while underwater.

He has been coaching for a long time and has rarely seen this ability. Daniel loves swimming and can briefly express his feelings about it. It's effortless for him and I'm in awe of him because I can't swim at all.

Swimming helps Daniel 'center" him and engages every part of his body. Since he started swimming, he has become more relaxed and in control. It's therapeutic and his overall behaviors have improved. He even sleeps better.

I would not have found out any of these things if I had not "stepped outside of my comfort zone" and tried new things with Daniel. That is my advice for all fathers dealing with their own special needs children. Don't be afraid to go against the expert advice.

Don't be fearful of what might happen when you place your child into non therapeutic environments. Treat your child "Like a Child" instead of a "special needs child" and watch what happens!

Ω

Use this section to reflect on what you have read thus far and how you can relate it to your own journey you're your own special needs children.

_____

_____

_____

_____

_____

_____

_____

_____

_____

_____

_____

_____

Thoroughly Immersed

TIP # 3:   Never   Be   Ashamed   of   or Embarrassed By your Child!

There have been many times in this journey of embracing and enjoying raising my "Special needs child" where I was frankly embarrassed by my child! It was when he was younger and we were just learning how to deal with his disorder.

I remember early on trying to take Daniel and the rest of the family to the movies. Daniel couldn't sit still for long periods of times because of his sensory issues. It didn't matter if we went to indoor or outdoor theatres. The same thing would occur. We couldn't enjoy the movie and were embarrassed when he started to cry and scream.

We would go out in public to the movies or restaurants and Daniel would begin to cry out uncontrollably. We didn't know what to do with him and usually we would be asked to leave. We didn't want to ruin the experience for other patrons. We had no answers and it was disruptive. It was uncomfortable to say the least.

When you have a special needs child, there are going to be some "uncomfortable moments"! We had to learn to adapt. We had to tell people ahead of time of his condition. But we also had to learn to develop an "I don't give a damn attitude".

Not everything is going to be "Atypical". But the purpose of these "gifts from GOD" as I call them is to help us be better as people! GOD sent these children to you to complete YOU! There are going to be some "trying" moments. Uneducated people are going to say things. Instead of being embarrassed by them, learn from them and their mannerisms. Use this time to work on creating a typical day for the child. Prepare your child's nerves for the day.

There was an incident at a NIKE store one day where Daniel reached out to another customer inappropriately. It had been an unusually long day for Daniel. In hindsight, I now recognize how that negatively impacts his behavior and boundaries. Daniel ran up to the man and startled him. Daniel was just saying hello in his own way, but it appeared aggressive to the unassuming customer. I was able to step in between the customer and Daniel to explain the situation to the customer.

This was an embarrassing situation, but it also was a teaching moment for me and for the customer. I was able to educate the customer on a child with autism and I also learned to be more keenly aware of Daniel's schedule and how he is affected by the length of or change in that schedule. I was also able to advocate for my child.

Dr. Amanda Carter: "It is important to become your child's greatest advocate to learn effective and appropriate treatment modalities and methodologies to integrate and implement in everyday life. Education and accessible resources are vital with this population because the more one knows about this particular topic the better informed decisions are made. More importantly, being vocal regarding the experiences and challenges of raising a child on the spectrum may potentially influence laws, policies, and heighten awareness."

I now know I have to look for signs of changes in Daniel's mood or behavior and look for the triggers that will cause the change, i.e. changes in time, changes in locations, changes in familiar places. I now know that Daniel needs to be "prompted" with brain activity throughout the day to keep him fresh and properly stimulated. That's where the activities like the swimming, the drum classes and the sports work well for him.

Parents of special needs children" must learn their child on much deeper level in order to avoid embarrassing moments and to be able to deal with them when they occur. Parents need to learn that it's OK despite these moments.

Parents, especially fathers, need to understand that within the mind of these children are violent noises that are taking place. These children cope with it much better than we ever could, but in a different manner.

Imagine being a person with sensory issues walking into a room and being able to hear "everything" that is going on; people talking, wind blowing, different tapping noises and every footstep taken. Sounds that "typical" people take for granted. Educating the public about what's happening with your child helps them to "see them" in a different manner and now you can advocate for your child on a deeper level.

So don't be embarrassed by or ashamed of your child. Love the "gift from GOD" given to you and learn to advocate for and educate others about children with special needs.

Ω

Use this section to reflect on what you have read thus far and how you can relate it to your own journey you're your own special needs children.

_____

_____

_____

_____

_____

_____

_____

_____

_____

_____

_____

Tip #4:   Be   Consistent   and   Avoid Spontaneity

Special needs children are dependent on routine schedules, more so than your typical child. They are prone to "meltdowns" if they don't have that consistency in their lives. Daniel is used to his swim classes and his drum lessons. If anyone of those things doesn't occur, he will "cry out" or "act out" in a negative way as a result. They need that structure on a daily basis or it can be a nightmare! These children thrive on motion and brain stimulation. That's what keeps them sharp. They got to MOVE!

Dr. Arnell Brady, Daniel's speech pathologist, was the first person that introduced Daniel to structured activities. He recommended the swimming and drum classes. Daniel has a 7 day schedule which includes the drumming, swimming, walking and other activities. Daniel, to our amazement, has had astonishing success in his drum classes and we often are brought to tears by what he can do. He has been able to learn intricate "drum cadences" in class and in swimming, he can hold his breath for an amazingly long time according to his swim instructor. We know this is therapeutic and a mental "massage for the mind." Daniel cannot articulate his schedule, but you can tell he is always ready to do his walking or drumming. Daniel is also in High school and that is incorporated into his schedule. Schedules for these children are always a "work in progress". But you can tell when he is off schedule by the changes in his behavior. On one occasion when he was off schedule, Daniel had a minor meltdown. Daniel is physically strong for his age and doesn't know his own strength. He is not intentionally violent, but when he has a meltdown, he will throw things and there will be screaming.

My advice to fathers is to start off slow. Start off with walking or some other type of physical activity. Constantly prompt them on correct posture and arm movements. Try to incorporate some type of musical instrument if they show an interest. Look into your local park district for activities the child can enroll in. Now please understand that this is "trial and error". All children are different and some things you try are not going to work out for your special needs child. Daniel has sensory issues, so some activities didn't work at first. But I kept looking for other activities and tried new things with him. Eventually, you will find what works for your child. Also don't be afraid to put them in activities with "regular education kids". Sometimes these sports or activities can be overwhelming but as their interactions improve, this can be a great outlet for your child to excel. Daniel has done well with some activities with general education kids such as swimming and wrestling. The key is to find a schedule that works for you and your child.

$$\Omega$$

Use this section to reflect on what you have read thus far and how you can relate it to your own journey you're your own special needs children.

_____

_____

_____

_____

Thoroughly Immersed

TIP # 5: Your Child Isn't PERFECT, but Neither Are You!

Many times in this journey of Enjoying and Embracing your "special needs child", other people may remind you that your child is not perfect. They will say less than pleasing things about your child. Sometimes you hear it, but sometime you don't. What has helped me in these moments is to go into "the chamber"; the quiet place where the outside noise cannot enter.

Parents of special needs children understand that their children will be viewed as different or less than perfect.

But that's ok because when you become "Thoroughly Immersed" in your child, nobody else matters but you, your child and your GOD! People will say things out of ignorance, fear or immaturity. It just doesn't matter and you as advocates for your child can either ignore the comments or use that moment to educate those people on autism and how it affects children like yours.

The other thing to recognize is that YOU are not perfect either! I believe the true purpose of any special needs child is to better the people around them in their lives. I remember watching a moving segment about a boxer who has a child with spinal bifida. That father is a different person because of her. She strengthens him and he is fighting for his special needs daughter!

They can empower you to a point that is unbelievable. They encourage you and strengthen you. I have become more humble and sensitive as a result of having this child. I have become more patient as a result of raising this child. They will capture your heart.

Your child watches you and learns from you. Daniel looks to me for guidance and direction. There will be times where you will disappoint your child, even if they cannot relay that information to you. Again, your child is not perfect and neither are you.

Don't expect that you are going to get it right every time and don't beat yourself up when that happens.

You are no different from the millions of other parents that occasionally disappoint their children or themselves in the course of raising them. Give yourself and your child a "break" and recognize perfection is something to reach for but rarely achieved.

$$\Omega$$

Use this section to reflect on what you have read thus far and how you can relate it to your own journey you're your own special needs children.

_____

_____

_____

_____

_____

_____

_____

_____

_____

_____

_____

Thoroughly Immersed

TIP#6:   Your Child is a "Treasure Chest" & Autism is the Padlock!

Every child has a gift and it is up to the parent to find out what it is. Once you are able to tap into that gift, there is no limits to where your child's gift may take him. It takes a parent who is "thoroughly immersed" in their child's life to find that gift or skill. One of my friends once told me that "autism" is nothing but "scattered genes".

Parents just need to pick one of them and capitalize on it. Autistic children have been found to have extraordinary abilities and have a "treasure chest" of gifts. According to the group, Autism Speaks, some of those abilities are:

Strong visual skills

■ Ability to understand and retain concrete concepts, rules, sequences and patterns

- Good memory of details or rote facts (math facts, train schedules, baseball statistics)

- Long-term memory

- Computer and technology skills

- Musical ability or interest

- Intense concentration or focus, especially on a preferred activity

- Artistic ability

- Mathematical ability

- Ability to decode written language (read) at an early age (but not necessarily comprehend)

- Strong encoding (spelling)

- Honesty

- Problem solving ability (when you cannot ask for something you want, you can get pretty creative about getting your hands on it yourself.)

Children with autism have heightened senses as well. They take in more than typical people can. Because their ability to communicate is deficient, their reflexes and other senses become heightened. My son Daniel is very skilled in swimming and it is one of the best physical activity an autistic child can be involved in. Daniel becomes "thoroughly immersed" in it to the point where he seems like every other typical boy. Swimming is therapeutic for him because he gets to utilize his entire body in the process. All of his senses are engaged in the act of swimming. It's soothing and I think in some cases it can take the place of medication. I believe that for every ailment or disability, there is an earthly solution or a physical activity to resolve it.

While Daniel would swim, his coach, Rudolph Henry, would discover he had an innate ability to breathe in the water, take in oxygen without gagging or choking, unlike most human beings. Similar to what you see with fish and their gills, this kind of phenomenon is only seen in humans during intro-uteri phase of pregnancy.

This is just the "tip of the iceberg" of what I will find out about Daniel and that is a message I want to share with all fathers. Your special needs child is wired differently from other typical children and therefore, there are varied treasures inside of them waiting to be found. But first, you have to find the key to unlock the treasure chest.

As mentioned earlier in the statistics from Autism Speaks, Daniel has also shown skills in the art of drumming, karate and football. All these skills are unique to him, not his parents. Neither of us were good swimmers nor are we musically inclined. His drum instructor was also moved to tears because of the success Daniel has shown.

Fathers, what is unique about your child? What skills, talents or gifts have you seen in your child? What can you do to continue to nurture and grow those abilities? If you are anything like me, you probably had no idea of what to look forward to in the life of your child once you received that dreadful diagnosis.

You could have never told me that Daniel would be a skilled swimmer or could learn how to play the drums. When you first get that diagnosis, it is utter devastation. But because he "came out of the world and got into the

WORD", we were able to dig into this treasure chest called Daniel! Fathers need to connect to their spirituality and realize their child is a "treasure" sent to you by GOD.

Ω

Use this section to reflect on what you have read thus far and how you can relate it to your own journey you're your own special needs children.

_____

_____

_____

_____

_____

_____

_____

_____

_____

_____

_____

Thoroughly Immersed

Thoroughly Immersed

Tip #7: Surround Your Self with Positivity

Fathers who lack support from family and friends must have alternative outlets and to avoid becoming tolerant of mental, emotional, and physical abuse. Thus, it is imperative to avoid enablement and seek available resources within the community and/or support groups in dealing with some of the day to day challenges of raising a child on the spectrum.

"Show me your friends and I'll show you your future."

That's a true statement because the people you associate with or hang around tend to show you your destiny.

Everyone needs positive people in their lives, especially fathers with special needs children. We constantly need to the positive energy of our friends and supporters to do what we do on a daily basis. We need to be encouraged and uplifted.

Most of my closest friends are men who not only embrace me, but my children as well. They speak

"LIFE" to my situation and Daniel's situation. Even though they can't verbalize it, children can sense positive and negative energy just like any other child and they want to be uplifted as well. When my friends come around, they embrace Daniel and treat him no different than they do my daughter or me.

My two fraternity brothers, Tom Gray & Tony Broadnack, come over often and show love to Daniel. Tom has told me on occasion that "Your son is a Genius! It's just scattered." There is so much sensory overload that it's hard for Daniel to process it all. Another of my friends told me that I had a blessed child because of the father I am. These positive expressions of support within my life are phenomenal and keep me going when times get rough on this journey to embracing and enjoying my special needs child.

As fathers, it's important for you to create a network of positive people you can call on at any time. Whether you find them in your neighborhood, at your place of worship, school or other autism support groups, make it a point to surround yourself with positivity.

Per Dr. Carter, Fathers who lack support from family and friends must have alternative outlets and to avoid becoming tolerant of mental, emotional, and physical abuse. Thus, it is imperative to avoid enablement and seek available resources within the community and/or support groups in dealing with some of the day to day challenges of raising a child on the spectrum.

Take time for you as well. Faith and Physical fitness are necessary. I'm 51 yrs old with a teenage son. So my workout has to be more intense than most because I may need to restrain him at any moment. I do a lot of weight lifting, boxing and cardiovascular training. I am meticulous in my diet as well. My child has forced me to be more cognizant of my own body as a result of being concerned about his physical limitations. I have to be in top shape mentally and physically so that I can be all I can be for him. Make sure you incorporate some physical activity into your own life. Go to the gym. Go bike riding or running.

My prayer life has grown because I understand that my son is a "gift from GOD" and I am a steward over this gift. I spoke of leaving the world and getting into the Word earlier and fathers need a strong prayer life to sustain them throughout the journey of raising their special needs child.

Not only is it important to find positivity and seek out encouragement, it is equally important to give encouragement to other fathers. The bible says, "Once you are convicted, you strengthen your brother" (Luke 22:32). If I could just help one dad, then I've done my job. It's my obligation to share with somebody else that is going thru what I'm going thru something that I've learned. I know there's got to be some man out there going thru what I've gone thru, but the enemy like to make us think we are alone in this fight.

There are mothers and celebrities like Jenny McCarthy and Holly Robinson-Peete that speak on national platforms about autism awareness and support for mothers. I want to speak and encourage the fathers of autistic children and be a support for them. Men are least likely to come out and express how they feel. They suffer in silence thinking that nobody cares.

I speak at support groups and fellowship with some men that are there. Fathers need to connect with autism support groups in their city like Autism Speaks.

$$\Omega$$

Use this section to reflect on what you have read thus far and how you can relate it to your own journey you're your own special needs children.

_____

_____

_____

_____

_____

_____

_____

_____

_____

Thoroughly Immersed

TIP#8:   **A Delay is not a DENIAL**

You can always dream for your child. I have high aspirations for Daniel and you never know what he will accomplish. I want him on top of the world as far as he can go. Fathers need to know that their child is a "work in progress" and they need to stay in the fight.

On the cover of this book, you can see a picture of Daniel at his 8th grade graduation. I had no idea this day would come when I got the diagnosis. I accepted the diagnosis, but didn't surrender to it! I accepted the diagnosis and then we went to work. I got more involved in his life and his therapy.

It wasn't until age ten that I was able to "Dream for him". I realized that if he was going to make it in this world, it was going to take more effort from me. Right now, we are embracing the whole child. We also are letting him know we love him and he can do anything. The important thing is for him to know he can do anything.

Fathers, you must Dream for your special need child and work with them to make the dream a reality. It may take longer than expected, but it will not be in vain. Your child is a treasure! Embrace them. Enjoy them. Raise them up to be all that they were created to be!

Consider this one last thought in closing. Is it possible that GOD would create your son before He created you, but allowed you to be born first? Is it possible that GOD allowed you to be born first so that He could mold you and shape you into the father your son would eventually need to embrace, enjoy and raise him?

I believe God had Daniel in mind for me long before I was created. I believe the same may be true for you as fathers of special needs children. These children are your ASSIGNMENTS. These children are your TREASURE.

Autism is just the temporary "padlock" waiting for you to figure out the right combination to unlock the treasure chests of your child's mind! You were created with the key that fits your child's lock. Embrace and Enjoy unlocking your child's and finding those treasures together!

Ω

Use this section to reflect on what you have read thus far and how you can relate it to your own journey you're your own special needs children.

_____

_____

_____

_____

_____

_____

_____

_____

_____

_____

_____

_____

_____

_____

_____

_____

_____

Thoroughly Immersed

People Who have been a part of Danny's and Daniel's Journey:

Mr. Rook

1. *What has been my working experience in working with Daniel?*

My experience working with Daniel was short but memorable. It was for extended school year and was only six weeks long. Upon his arrival at my school, Daniel was placed in another classroom before he came to mine.

He was having difficulty adjusting to the new learning environment so they moved him into my room. The first few days were rocky, since it was a new school, new teacher, new schedule and new routine for Daniel. But once Daniel became acclimated to the learning environment and the structure of the room, he fit right it in.

He did occasionally test his boundaries to determine what was acceptable and unacceptable, but all he needed was a redirect to get him to focus on his own tasks and responsibilities.

2. *My impression of Danny's work and relationship with Daniel*

The time and dedication you devote to your son is incredible. When working with students with Autism, the need to have set rules, schedules, and routines is crucial. In the case of Daniel, his schedule is going to the gym, school, and wrestling.

This type of structure is what students with Autism need to function. They thrive on repetition and routine. This will benefit him greatly later in life not only with self-management, but socially as well.

Students with Autism also often exhibit sensory and fine motor delays. Teaching Daniel to exercise using weights, swimming, gymnastics, and wrestling is a unique, fun and successful approach to addressing these sensory deficits.
In these activities, Daniel has to use his senses and fine motor skills to complete tasks which teach him to better regulate his body.

Coach Rudolph Henry

I have been working with Danny for several years. My background and professional training is that of an educator working with children with special needs for 40 plus and a swim instructor for 45 plus years. We also had a private therapeutic day school for 15 years. I have had the opportunity to meet and interact with many parents and clinicians over the years of best practices for servicing children with special needs. When it came to those who were autistic and where they were on the spectrum of autism, opinions differed as to the best practices for treatment. Treatment varied from drugs to hospitalization to being institutionalized. I commend this dad for not accepting the easy way out.

His steadfast determination to seek alternative avenues to help his son to grow socially is astounding. Don't get me wrong it has not been without challenges. Ok, I will add this one important fact that makes all of this so amazing. He has done it without the reliance of drugs! We will continue to monitor his journey of being exposed to many different activities to enhance his social growth.

Biographies:

Daniel "aka Danny" Randall

Danny is a Husband, Father of 2, well respected Chicago Police Officer and an advocate for autism. He works tirelessly with his son, Daniel, to keep him engaged and motivated as he walks this journey.

Danny is very active in his efforts to support and promote new nontraditional therapies or treatments that will improve the lives of people who live with autism in all its forms today. Danny believes in incorporating "whole body movement "and "Aggressive Mainstreaming via Sports" into traditional therapy. He has seen it work wonders with his own son.

He is widely known as an advocate for Fathers of children with autism and neurological differences. He wants to help them find their voice, increase awareness about how fathers everywhere "suffer in silence" with this issue and help them go from "embarrassment to enjoyment" of their children.

In addition to his autism advocacy work, Danny is a member of Omega Psi Phi Fraternity, INC. He also is a member of New Life Covenant Church in Chicago where Pastor John F. Hannah presides. He was born and raised in Chicago, IL. And still lives there with his wife Beryl, daughter Danielle and son Daniel.

Terrance "The Unstoppable Coach" Leftridge

Terrance "The Unstoppable Coach" Leftridge has had a desire to help people, empower people and entertain them his whole life. Terrance is at his best in front of an audience. His intent is to always leave people better off than before they met him.

Terrance is a Certified Accountability Coach. He is the founder of UNSTOPPABLE Coaching Services Inc. where the #1 Goal is to help his clients Live Life on the Next Level by partnering with them on their journey to creating, implementing and achieving their visions.

He has worked with men and women who are transitioning from working traditional jobs and helped them start successful careers in entrepreneurship. He teaches them how to be better marketers, better networkers and build stronger relationships that lead to greater exposure and more sales! Throughout his professional career as a coach, Terrance has had a passion for encouraging and motivating people to move to the Next Level of their Greatness.

He has spoken at Live and virtual seminars and training events across the country. He utilizes his internet broadcast, "The Next Level Living Show with Coach Terrance" as a platform to expose his guests to a larger audience and as a result increase their circle of influence and generate leads.

For more information on booking Terrance for your next event or speaking engagement, contact him at Terrance@unstoppablecoaching.com

DR. AMANDA M. CARTER, CEO AND FOUNDER OF CARAFAP, LLC

Dr. Amanda Carter was born in Washington, D.C., and an only child who was raised in Maryland. She attended Shaw University located in Raleigh, North Carolina for undergraduate studies and successfully completed the required course work in three years with honors with a major in Psychology. She obtained her Master's at Howard University in Washington,

D.C. Subsequently, she enrolled into a Doctoral program at Argosy University for two semesters and transferred to Nova Southeastern University located in Fort Lauderdale, Florida. In June 2014, she graduated with a Doctoral degree maintaining a GPA of 3.96. Her dissertation was conducted in East Haddam, Connecticut which addressed Parental Perceptions for Adolescents diagnosed with Asperser's Syndrome and/or Autism Spectrum Disorder. Additionally, Dr. Carter will receive an honorary doctorate on February 19, 2016 from Global Oved Dei Seminary University for her outstanding and commendable work towards the autistic population. She was also selected as the Valedictorian for the upcoming graduation.

Dr. Carter's area of expertise includes Autism Spectrum Disorder, and mental health. In November 2014, Dr. Carter founded her own organization, Care and Recreational Activities for Autistic People (CARAFAP, LLC). The mission of CARAFAP, LLC is to provide recreational, respite, special events, behavioral, and consulting services for individuals diagnosed with Autism Spectrum Disorder and Down Syndrome. CARAFAP's goal is to create a supportive environment where individuals with disabilities are free to be themselves without being pigeonholed by societal norms and expectations. Additionally, CARAFAP offers non-traditional therapies which include incorporation of animals, music, and art therapy in an effort to create supportive environments to enhance an individual's motivational interest. Dr. Carter's organization conducted a recreational and resource fair on

October 31, 2015 located in Newport News, Virginia to serve families with children diagnosed with Autism and Down Syndrome. Service dogs and horses were also featured during this event.

In January and March of 2015, Dr. Carter was selected to participate in a live Poly Com conference on national television. She won an award in May 2015 for being a thriving entrepreneur at the Bold, Brave, and Beautiful Award ceremony, Dr. Carter was featured on "The Soul of A Woman" international radio show in August 2015. She was also featured on WTKR News Station in October 2015. Dr. Carter continues to accept televised opportunities to educate the world about CARAFAP's services and autism.

In addition, Dr. Carter serves as a community ambassador with Autism Speaks in an effort to increase awareness and raise funds for individuals diagnosed with autism. She has coordinated and participated in 5k events for children diagnosed with autism. Dr. Carter is a member of Empowerment Temple located in Baltimore, Maryland and is working to establish a ministry for special needs.

Dr. Carter is currently raising a service dog to help aid in the lives of children diagnosed with developmental and intellectual disabilities. She enjoys riding horses, reading, traveling, and spending time with her family.

Made in the USA
San Bernardino, CA
29 May 2016